Oxford Read and Discover

Discover! 5

Great Migrations

Rachel Bladon

Contents

OXFORD
UNIVERSITY PRESS

OXFORD
UNIVERSITY PRESS

Great Clarendon Street, Oxford OX2 6DP

Oxford University Press is a department of the University of Oxford. It furthers the University's objective of excellence in research, scholarship, and education by publishing worldwide in

Oxford New York

Auckland Cape Town Dar es Salaam Hong Kong Karachi Kuala Lumpur Madrid Melbourne Mexico City Nairobi New Delhi Shanghai Taipei Toronto

With offices in

Argentina Austria Brazil Chile Czech Republic France Greece Guatemala Hungary Italy Japan Poland Portugal Singapore South Korea Switzerland Thailand Turkey Ukraine Vietnam

OXFORD and OXFORD ENGLISH are registered trade marks of Oxford University Press in the UK and in certain other countries

© Oxford University Press 2010

The moral rights of the author have been asserted

Database right Oxford University Press (maker)

First published 2010

2014 2013 2012

10 9 8 7 6 5 4

No unauthorized photocopying

ISBN: 978 0 19 464501 0

An Audio CD Pack containing this book and a CD is also available, ISBN 978 0 19 464541 6

The CD has a choice of American and British English recordings of the complete text.

An accompanying Activity Book is also available, ISBN 978 0 19 464511 9

Printed in China

This book is printed on paper from certified and well-managed sources.

ACKNOWLEDGEMENTS

Illustrations by: Kelly Kennedy pp.19, 30; Dusan Pavlic/Beehive Illustration pp.40, 45, 48; Mark Ruffle pp.5, 8, 9, 17, 20, 24, 38.

The Publishers would also like to thank the following for their kind permission to reproduce photographs and other copyright material: Alamy pp.5 (B.A.E. Inc.), 6 (Jack Milchanowski/ Papilio), 12 (Danita Delimont), 33 (Blickwinkel); Corbis pp.3 (Frans Lanting/ elephants), 7 (Frans Lanting), 14 (Pierre Holtz/ Reuters), 16 (Nik Wheeler), 19 (John Van Hasselt/ Sygma), 22 (Frans Lanting), 24 (Dennis Scott); Getty Images pp.13 (George Lapp), 23 (Bobby Haas/ National Geographic), 25 (Daisy Gilardini/ The Image Bank), 26 (Paul Sutherland/ National Geographic), 29 (John Warden/ Stone), 31 (Bill Curtsinger/ National Geographic/baby turtles); Nature Picture Library pp.3 (Inaki Relanzon/sea turtle, Mark Taylor/albatross, Peter Scoones/salmon), 4 (Steve Knell), 10 (Aflo/geese), 11 (Tom Hugh-Jones), 15 (Mark Carwardine), 21 (Anup Shah), 27 (Constantinos Petrinos), 28 (Peter Scoones), 30 (Jane Burton), 31 (Inaki Relanzon/sea turtle), 32 (Mark Taylor); Oxford University Press p.17; Photolibrary pp.9 (Ted Mead), 10 (Tobias Bernhard/sooty shearwater), 18 (Peter Lilia); Still Pictures pp.34 (Biosphoto/ Vernay Pierre/ Polar Lys), 35 (J. Freund/WILDLIFE).

With thanks to: Ann Fullick for science checking

Introduction

Around the world, day and night, and in every season, animals are moving from one place to another. They move over land, in the air, or through water. Some make short journeys, others go across the world. These animals are all migrating. Animal migrations are amazing.

What animals can you see below?

Why do animals migrate?

How do animals find their way when they migrate?

What animal has made the longest migration?

What animals migrate to or from your country?

Now read and discover more about some great animal migrations!

3

On the Move

Migration is when animals move from one place to another. Sometimes huge numbers of animals migrate together, but some animals migrate thousands of kilometers all alone.

Why Do Animals Migrate?

Many places are not good for animals to live in all year long. The places are sometimes too cold or hot, or not good for baby animals. Sometimes there is not enough food. Animals have to move away for part of the year or for part of their lives. They migrate to find food, water, and a safe place to live or breed.

Sometimes all the animals in a species migrate. This is called complete migration. If only some animals in a species migrate, it's called partial migration.

An Arctic Tern

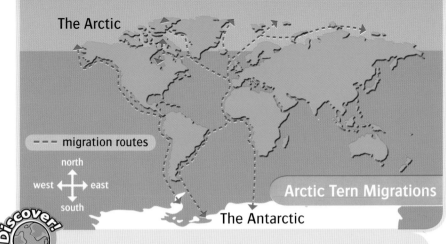

The Arctic

--- migration routes

north
west ←→ east
south

Arctic Tern Migrations

The Antarctic

Discover!

Arctic terns migrate from the Arctic to the Antarctic and back every year. That's almost 50,000 kilometers!

When To Go

Animals that migrate are called migrants. Many migrants leave their home at the same time every year. They reach the end of their journey at about the same time, too. So how do they know when it is time to leave? Animals see things in the world around them that tell them to leave. The days get longer or shorter. The weather gets hotter or colder, or there is less food to eat. Scientists think that when migrants see that these things are changing, their bodies make special chemicals called hormones. The hormones make an animal eat lots of food so that it has enough energy for its journey.

Swallows Ready to Migrate

Finding Their Way

Animals are very good at finding their way. Some use landmarks – important places that they can see, for example, mountains and coasts. Others use the sun during the day, or the moon and stars at night. Some animals use smells to help them to find their way. Scientists think that some animals can even feel Earth's magnetic field and use it to tell them where they are. It's like the animals have a compass inside.

An Insect-Eating Bat

Discover!

Some animals, like bats and whales, make special sounds when they are moving. The echoes from these sounds help them to find their way.

Dangers

Migrating is often dangerous. The journey is very tiring for animals, and they sometimes find it difficult to get food and water. They are in danger from bad weather and predators – other animals that want to kill and eat them. There are many dangers, but these do not stop migrants. They have to make long journeys to find safe places to breed and a home with lots of food!

Lions Hunting Zebras

Go to pages 36–37 for activities.

Bird Migrations

There are many different species of bird, and about half of them migrate. Some birds only travel a few kilometers, but others go all the way around the world!

Where Do Birds Migrate?

In the northern half of the world, days are long in summer, and birds can easily find food for their young. In winter, many of these birds fly south because it's too cold in the north and there is not enough food. Birds in the southern half of the world fly north for winter and back south for summer.

Many birds also migrate between east and west, usually looking for warmer winter weather near the ocean. Most birds in the Tropics do not migrate because it's always warm there.

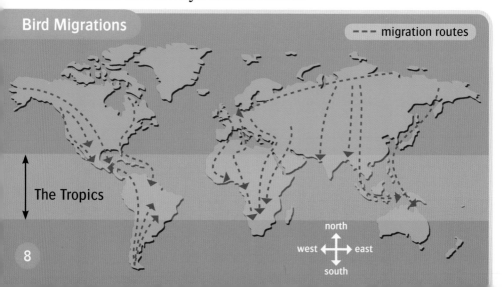

Bird Migrations

--- migration routes

The Tropics

north
west ←┼→ east
south

Discover!

Bar-tailed godwits from New Zealand fly further without stopping than any other bird. They fly 11,500 kilometers to China. Then after feeding, they fly another 5,000 kilometers to Alaska to breed!

- - - migration routes

Alaska

CHINA

NEW ZEALAND

Getting Ready

Before birds migrate, they need to eat a lot of food so that they have enough energy for their journey. Some birds double their weight before migrating. Their muscles become stronger, too. Before migrating, many birds also molt – they lose their old feathers and new ones grow. They wait for good weather, and then they are ready to go!

A sooty shearwater from New Zealand flew 64,000 kilometers in 2005. This was the longest animal migration ever recorded.

Learning Where To Go

Many large water birds, like geese and cranes, learn where to go from their parents or other older birds. They also have to learn the best way to fly. Geese and cranes always fly in a V-shape because the air from the wings of the bird at the front helps the other birds to fly.

Geese Flying in a V-Shape

Whooping Cranes
Following a Plane

Whooping cranes
in the USA almost
became extinct – this means
that there were very few birds of
that species left. In 1999, scientists
brought some young whooping cranes to
Florida in the south of the USA. Whooping
cranes lived here many years before, and always
migrated to Wisconsin in the north of the USA.
The new young cranes could not learn this from
their parents, so the scientists had to teach them. The
scientists flew to Wisconsin in special planes. Because
the scientists made the cranes listen to the sound of
the planes when they were in the egg, the cranes
followed them!

Dangers

There are many dangers for migrating birds. Hunters
often wait for them because they know where and
when they will fly. Tall buildings, like skyscrapers and
wind turbines, kill many migrating birds. Also, because
of farming or building, many birds lose their habitats
– the places where they stop or migrate to.

Go to pages 38–39 for activities.

Insect and Bat Migrations

Many species of insect, like dragonflies, butterflies, and locusts, make short or long migrations by air. Many species of bat also migrate by flying.

Dragonflies

Dragonflies live underwater for most of their lives, as larvae. Then they become adults – they climb out of the water, their old skin comes off, and their wings slowly open. Dragonflies only live for a few months as adults, but some species migrate. They use the wind to carry them to warmer habitats in the fall.

Discover!

Green darner dragonflies weigh less than 2 grams, but some migrate all the way across the Atlantic Ocean.

Monarch Butterflies on a Tree

Monarch Butterflies

Every fall, millions of monarch butterflies from North America fly up to 3,000 kilometers south to Mexico. Here, they rest and sleep in trees for the winter months. Then, when spring comes, they fly back to North America. They breed before they die.

The migration of the monarch butterflies is beautiful, and it's also amazing. Because monarch butterflies live for less than a year, no butterfly ever makes the same journey again. The monarch butterflies that leave North America have never flown south to Mexico before, but they know where to go. Every year, millions of new butterflies move north and south, going the same way every time and resting in the same trees.

Desert Locusts

Desert locusts migrate when there are too many locusts in one place. This is called irruptive migration. Desert locusts usually live alone, and they only move around at night. When there are too many locusts, the young locusts change color, and they change how they live. During the day they fly around in large groups called swarms. They travel up to 200 kilometers every day to find new places with food and fewer locusts.

A locust swarm can have up to one billion locusts. A locust can eat its own weight in food every day, so thousands of people starve every year when locust swarms eat food crops.

Bats

In places that get cold in winter, there are fewer insects, so many species of insect-eating bat migrate. Some bats make only short journeys, but others migrate more than 1,000 kilometers.

Every year, during the wet season when there is a lot of rain, millions of fruit bats in Africa migrate to Kasanka National Park in Zambia. At this time, there is lots of fruit on the trees. At night, the bats feed on the fruit, and then at dawn, they fly into forests where they rest and sleep. They eat as much as 5,000 metric tons of fruit every night.

Fruit Bats

Go to pages 40–41 for activities.

4 Migrations by Land

When animals migrate by land, they do not have help from the wind or ocean currents. Their journeys are often shorter than air or ocean migrations, but the animals sometimes have to cross deserts, mountains, or ice.

Reindeer

Reindeer are a species of deer that live in the Arctic. They are called caribou in North America. They make longer migrations than any other land animal. Some reindeer walk more than 4,000 kilometers every year. Because they live in large groups, or herds, they quickly eat up food and then they have to move to another place.

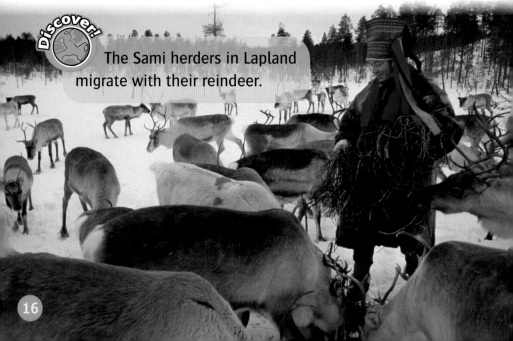

Discover!

The Sami herders in Lapland migrate with their reindeer.

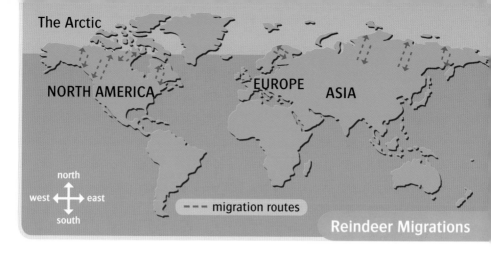

The Arctic

NORTH AMERICA   EUROPE   ASIA

north
west ←✛→ east
south

- - - migration routes

Reindeer Migrations

In summer, the reindeer move north, or into the mountains, where they can find good grass to eat. They can feed their young here, too. They are also safer because they can see predators like bears and wolves, and they can escape from them more easily.

In winter, when the snow is deep, the reindeer move to places where there is less snow, so they can find lichens to eat. Reindeer stop growing in winter, so they need up to 70% less food than in summer.

Altitudinal Migration

Chamois, deer, wild sheep, and goats move up mountains in summer because there are fewer predators. In winter, there is too much snow and not enough food, so they move down the mountains. This is called altitudinal migration.

A Chamois

17

A Norway Lemming

Lemmings

When there is a lot of food, Norway lemmings breed very quickly – they can have up to eight babies every month. Then there are too many lemmings, and not enough for them to eat, so large numbers of young lemmings migrate a long way to find food. They even try to swim across rivers and lakes to find a new place to live with lots of food. Many die, but the lemmings keep having more new babies.

Because our climate is changing, there are fewer big lemming migrations now.

Frogs and Toads

Every year, frogs and toads migrate from their homes on the land to water where they can breed. They only move about 1 or 2 kilometers, but their journeys are very dangerous. They can die if they become too hot or dry, and it's easy for predators to find them when they are migrating. Many frogs and toads are also killed if they have to cross roads to get to the places where they breed.

Discover!

In some countries, people build special tunnels or stop cars so that frogs and toads can cross roads safely!

Mataranka 76
Katherine 178
Darwin 492

Toads Crossing a Road

Go to pages 42–43 for activities.

5 Migrations in Africa

Some of the most amazing animals in the world live in Africa. How many African animals can you think of? Do you know if they migrate?

The Wildebeest Migration

On the African plains, there is a wet season and a dry season every year. All year long, herds of wildebeest move across the plains in Tanzania and Kenya looking for fresh grass. There are more than a million wildebeest. The animals follow the rain, so their movements are different every year, but the journey takes them in a big circle from the Masai Mara National Park in the north down to the Serengeti National Park in the south – up to 3,000 kilometers. At the Serengeti, where the grass is very good in the wet season, the wildebeest have their young.

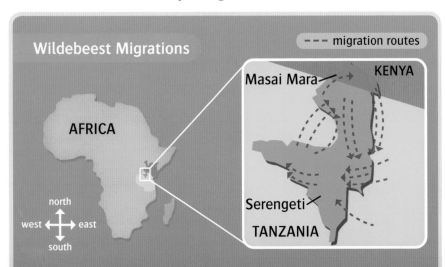

Wildebeest Migrations

- - - migration routes

AFRICA

Masai Mara
KENYA

Serengeti

TANZANIA

north
west ⟷ east
south

Discover!

About 200,000 zebras and 500,000 gazelles also migrate with the herds of wildebeest.

Wildebeest and Zebras

Dangers

There are many dangers for the migrating wildebeest, zebras, and gazelles. Predators, like lions, leopards, and hyenas, want to kill and eat the herds. The animals also have to cross big rivers. If the rains have been heavy, the rivers are sometimes very dangerous, and many animals die. Crocodiles attack the herds, too. Also, people are using more and more land for growing food, so there is less land for the herds to move around on – and less grass for them to eat.

21

Elephants

Elephants migrate to look for food and water. Male elephants also make long migrations to look for a mate – a female elephant to breed with. For most of the year, male elephants eat and make their bodies strong. Then they have a special time of year, called *musth*, when they migrate hundreds of kilometers to find a mate. They have to fight other male elephants, too. So when they come back after mating they are very thin, and they have little energy.

Discover! An adult elephant needs about 100 kilograms of food every day, and up to 300 liters of water. So for about 80% of the day, elephants feed or look for food.

Giraffes in the Okavango Floods

The Okavango Delta

The Okavango Delta is in the Kalahari Desert in Botswana in Africa. For six months it's dry and sandy, and nothing grows here. Then every summer, it floods, and grass covers the land. When the water comes, many birds and other animals migrate here. Dragonflies, cranes, deer, buffaloes, elephants, giraffes, and many other animals all migrate to the Okavango Delta to look for food and water.

→ Go to pages 44–45 for activities.

Many fish migrate around the ocean, and some ocean mammals migrate, too. Some make very long journeys.

A Humpback Whale

Whales

Many whales, like humpback whales and gray whales, migrate to polar oceans in summer. Here they can find lots of their favorite food, krill. Young whales cannot keep warm enough in very cold oceans, so in winter, the whales migrate back to warmer, tropical oceans to breed.

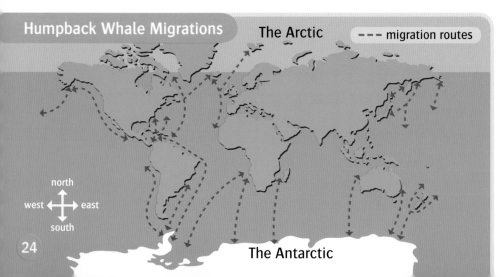

Humpback Whale Migrations   The Arctic   - - - migration routes

north
west ← → east
south

The Antarctic

Humpback whales migrate further than any other mammal – up to 17,000 kilometers every year. They migrate for the first time with their mothers, and then they usually make the same journey every year for the rest of their lives. During their journeys, humpback whales make special sounds, like a song. All humpback whales in the same part of the world sing almost the same song, and it changes every year!

Emperor Penguins

In summer in the Antarctic, emperor penguins hunt for krill, fish, and squid in the ocean. In March, when the ice gets thicker, adult penguins migrate up to 200 kilometers across the ice to their breeding places. After the females have laid their eggs, they go back to the ocean to feed. The males keep the eggs warm on their feet. They often have to wait for up to 16 weeks for the eggs to hatch, and they do not eat during this time.

Discover!

Penguins cannot walk well, so they often push themselves across the ice on their stomachs.

stomach

25

Bluefin Tuna

Fish

Some fish move away from coral reefs at night to feed. Then they go back there in the day because they can hide easily from predators under the coral. Other reef fish make longer migrations to breed. They lay their eggs near the edge of the reef, so that ocean currents will carry the eggs away from predators. Some bigger fish, like tuna, make very long journeys of up to 10,500 kilometers between the places where they feed and breed.

Vertical Migrations

Animal plankton are very small animals that live in the ocean. Every day, they make vertical migrations – they migrate up and down. They move up the ocean at night, to eat plant plankton that live at the top of the ocean. Then they move down the ocean in the day. Jellyfish, squid, and small fish that eat plankton migrate up and down the ocean with them. Bigger animals, like sharks, dolphins, and sea turtles, eat the small fish, so they follow, too. Every day, billions of animals move up and down the ocean.

Squid

→ Go to pages 46–47 for activities.

7 Going Home to Breed

Many animals migrate to breed. Some make long and difficult journeys to get to special breeding places.

Salmon

Most water animals live either in salt water or in fresh water. Salmon are unusual. Salmon eggs hatch in freshwater streams and then the salmon migrate down rivers to the ocean. When they get to the ocean, salmon often make long journeys to places where there is lots of food. They stay in the ocean for up to six years. Amazingly, the salmon then swim back up rivers into the streams where they hatched. Some salmon travel hundreds of kilometers. They use smell to find their way home. They go back to breed, and most species of salmon then die.

Before sockeye salmon breed, they change color from silver to red.

A Bear Hunting Salmon

Dangers for Salmon

It's tiring and dangerous for salmon to migrate up rivers, because the water moves them in the opposite direction. Because salmon usually migrate at the same time each year, many predators, like birds, bigger fish, and bears, wait for them. Salmon are also in danger when trees are cut down, or when rivers are polluted, because this damages their habitats. Dams can stop salmon migrating, or they can kill or hurt them. Dams are often built with fish ladders so that salmon can jump up from pool to pool.

Eels

Eels migrate from fresh water to salt water to have their young. Eel larvae move across the ocean with ocean currents, and young eels then migrate up rivers and streams. After many years in rivers, the eels grow into adults. Then they migrate back to the ocean to breed. They become silver so that they are hidden from ocean predators. Some eels migrate up to 8,000 kilometers across the ocean before breeding.

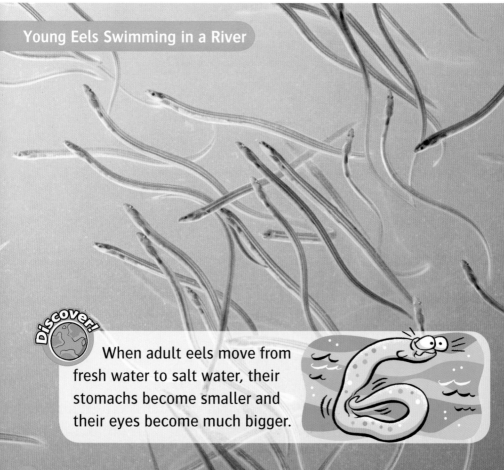

Young Eels Swimming in a River

Discover!

When adult eels move from fresh water to salt water, their stomachs become smaller and their eyes become much bigger.

Sea Turtles

Sea turtles migrate thousands of kilometers to breed. Scientists think that many turtles go back every year to the same place to lay their eggs. How do they know where to go? Scientists think that they follow Earth's magnetic field. The turtles lay their eggs on land, and they cover them with sand. They then swim away to the places where they feed. When the eggs hatch, the young turtles dig their way out of the sand. They then go to the ocean and swim away.

Young Sea Turtles Going to the Ocean

Go to pages 48–49 for activities.

8 Changing Migrations

Animals that migrate move through different habitats and they need different types of food in different places. Because of this, they are in danger from things that change in the world around them.

Problems for Migrants

Many migrants, like tuna, cod, birds, and sea turtles, are in danger from too much fishing or hunting. Roads, power lines, and wind turbines stop other animals from migrating. Also, people damage the habitats of many migrants when they cut down trees, take out ponds, build dams across rivers, or build fences around land. Pollution damages habitats, too.

Discover!

Every year, about 100,000 albatrosses are killed by fishing hooks.

The Climate is Changing

Earth is getting too warm because our vehicles, factories, and power stations are making too many gases like carbon dioxide. The climate is changing, so there are more storms, and deserts are getting bigger. There is less ice on polar oceans, and ocean currents are changing.

Journeys are now more dangerous for migrants. It's also more difficult for animals to reach the right place at the right time for feeding and breeding. Scientists think that many animal species will stop migrating or they will migrate to new places because the climate is changing.

Discover!

Many birds that migrate north for summer, like the willow warbler, are now staying there for longer than usual. Some birds are not migrating back south.

Polar Bears in Danger

Polar bears live on the ice in the Arctic in winter. Here they can hunt seals, their main food. In summer, there is not enough ice for hunting, so polar bears migrate south to the land. Because the climate is changing, there is now less ice on the ocean, and the ice is melting earlier in spring. So in winter, the bears have less time on the ice for catching seals. Also, it's sometimes difficult for the bears to migrate to land because there is less ice to walk on and they often have to swim too far across the ocean.

A Polar Bear on Melting Ice

How Can We Help?

Scientists are now putting special markers on some migrants. These markers help scientists to see where the animals are migrating, and how their journeys are changing. Scientists hope that if they learn more about migrants, they can help to save their habitats.

A Christmas Island Crab with a Marker

Discover! In the wet season on Christmas Island in Asia, millions of red crabs migrate to the ocean to breed. Markers have helped scientists to learn about their migration.

We need to keep our planet Earth clean and safe to protect animal migrations!

→ Go to pages 50–51 for activities.

1 On the Move

← Read pages 4–7.

1 Complete the chart.

> chemicals hotter bad weather sounds ~~food~~ sun
> longer water breed food landmarks moon live stars
> Earth's magnetic field smells shorter colder predators

1 Animals migrate to find:

___food___ and _____

a safe place to _____ or _____

2 Animals know when to migrate because:

the days get _____ or _____

the weather gets _____ or _____

there is less _____

their bodies make special _____

3 To find their way, animals use:

_____ _____ _____

_____ _____ _____

_____

4 When animals migrate, there are dangers from:

_____ or _____

2 **Match.**

1 migration
2 migrant
3 complete migration
4 partial migration
5 predators

animals that kill and eat other animals

when only some animals in a species migrate

when all the animals in a species migrate

when animals move from one place to another

an animal that migrates

3 **Correct the sentences.**

1 If a place is not good all year long, animals often breed.

   If a place is not good all year long, animals often migrate.

2 Arctic terns migrate from the Arctic to the Antarctic and back every week.

   _____

3 Some animals can feel Earth's magnetic garden.

   _____

4 Zebras and whales make special sounds when they are moving.

   _____

5 The smells from these sounds help them to find their way.

   _____

② Bird Migrations

← Read pages 8–11.

1 Write the places.

> Wisconsin   Florida   China   ~~New Zealand~~   Alaska

1 <u>New Zealand</u>

2 _____

3 _____

4 _____

5 _____

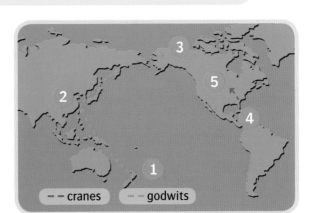

-- cranes   -- godwits

2 Complete the sentences.

> east   Tropics   north   south   north   west   ~~south~~

1 Many birds from the northern half of the world fly

   ___south___ for winter and back _____ for summer.

2 In the southern half of the world, many birds fly

   _____ for winter and back _____ for summer.

3 Other birds migrate between _____ and _____
   because in winter it is usually warmer near the ocean.

4 Most birds in the _____ do not migrate.

3 Match.

1 Bar-tailed godwits
2 Bar-tailed godwits
3 Geese and cranes
4 Geese and cranes
5 Whooping cranes
6 Whooping cranes

learn where to go from their parents.

fly further without stopping than any other bird.

fly in a V-shape.

almost became extinct in the USA.

fly 11,500 kilometers without stopping.

have learned to migrate by following planes.

4 Answer the questions.

1 Why do some birds fly south for winter?

Because it's too cold and there is not enough food.

2 Why do birds fly north for summer?

3 What things often happen to birds before they migrate?

4 What do birds wait for before they migrate?

5 What things are dangerous for migrating birds?

3 Insect and Bat Migrations

← Read pages 12–15.

1 Complete the sentences. Then write the numbers.

> old skin ~~larvae~~ habitats

1 Dragonflies live underwater as ___larvae___ .

2 When they become adults, their _____ comes off and their wings open.

3 Then they fly away to find warmer _____ .

> eggs trees south

4 Every fall, monarch butterflies fly _____ to Mexico.

5 They rest and sleep in _____ for the winter.

6 In spring, they fly north, lay their _____ , and die.

2 Circle the correct words.

1 Dragonflies migrate to warmer habitats in **fall** / **spring**.

2 Green darner dragonflies weigh **less** / **more** than 2 grams.

3 Every fall, **millions** / **thousands** of monarch butterflies fly up to 3,000 kilometers to Mexico.

4 A locust can eat as much food as the weight of its own **wings** / **body**.

5 Insect-eating bats migrate for the **winter** / **summer** because there is not enough food.

3 Match.

1 larvae

2 irruptive migration

3 wet season

4 swarms

when animals move away because there are too many in one place

the rainy time in the Tropics

large groups of insects

baby animals that change when they become adults

4 Answer the questions.

1 Why do monarch butterflies only migrate once?

_____

2 How do locusts change when there are too many locusts?

_____

3 How far do some insect-eating bats migrate?

_____

4 When do fruit bats migrate to Kasanka National Park?

_____

Migrations by Land

← Read pages 16–19.

1 Match. Then write the sentences.

Reindeer	migrate to new places when there are too many of them.
Lemmings	migrate to water to breed.
Frogs and toads	migrate in big herds to find grass and lichens.

1 _____

2 _____

3 _____

2 Complete the sentences.

grow   Arctic   north   deer   snow   grass   lichens

1 Reindeer are a species of _____. They live in the

_____ .

2 In summer, the reindeer move _____ where they can

find _____ .

3 In winter, the reindeer move to places where there is less

_____ , so they can find _____ .

4 Reindeer do not _____ in winter so they need less

food.

3 Answer the questions.

1 Why do reindeer eat up the food in each place so quickly?

_____

2 Why do goats move up mountains in summer?

_____

3 Why do goats move down mountains in winter?

_____

4 Why do lemmings sometimes swim across rivers and lakes?

_____

4 Complete the puzzle.

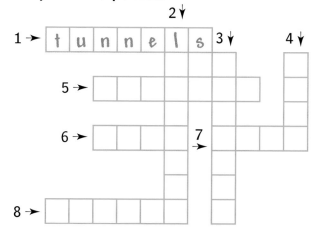

1 They help frogs and toads to cross roads safely.
2 Animals that can have up to eight babies every month.
3 Plants that reindeer eat in winter.
4 An animal that dies if it becomes too hot or dry.
5 Animals that make altitudinal migrations.
6 Reindeer herders who migrate with their animals.
7 A large group of animals.
8 Predators that attack reindeer.

Migrations in Africa

← Read pages 20–23.

1 Write the numbers.

> 300   200,000   ~~one~~   100   500,000   six   80   3,000

1 More than ____one____ million wildebeest migrate in herds across the African plains.

2 The wildebeest migrate up to _____ kilometers every year.

3 About _____ zebras and _____ gazelles migrate, too.

4 An adult elephant needs about _____ kilograms of food every day, and up to _____ liters of water.

5 Elephants feed or look for food for about _____ % of the day.

6 The Okavango Delta is dry and sandy for _____ months of the year.

2 Find and write the animals.

1 _giraffe_   5 _l_____

2 _z_____   6 _b_____

3 _h_____   7 _c_____

4 _g_____   8 _l_____

a	k	l	i	o	n	z	d
g	i	r	a	f	f	e	b
a	e	l	b	e	g	b	u
z	i	p	s	i	m	r	f
e	r	h	y	e	n	a	f
l	c	n	f	o	h	j	a
l	e	o	p	a	r	d	l
e	c	c	r	a	n	e	o

3 Complete the sentences. Then write the numbers.

> thin fight eat migrate

1 For most of the year, male elephants _____ and make their bodies strong.

2 Then they _____ to find female elephants to mate with.

3 They have to _____ other male elephants.

4 When they come back after mating they are very _____ .

4 Circle the correct words.

1 Wildebeest migrate to follow the **rain** / **lions**.

2 They migrate from the Masai Mara in the **north** / **south** to the Serengeti in the **north** / **south**.

3 They have their young in the **Masai Mara** / **Serengeti**.

4 Many wildebeest die when they cross big **rivers** / **oceans**.

5 Because people are growing more food on the land, there is less **rain** / **grass** for the wildebeest.

6 **Female** / **Male** elephants migrate to look for a mate.

7 *Musth* is a special time when male elephants want to **eat** / **find a mate**.

8 Birds and other animals migrate to the Okavango Delta in summer because there is lots of **sand** / **grass**.

6 Ocean Migrations

1 Complete the chart.

Name: _humpback whale_

Favorite food: _____

Lives (summer): _____

Lives (winter): _____

Amazing facts: _____

_____

2 Write the animal words.

1 d$_u$qs_i _____squid_____

2 p$_i$$_n$h^{o}l$_d$ _____

3 g^{un}p^{in}e _____

4 a^n$_{ut}$ _____

5 ta^n$_n$kl^{o}p _____

6 ^{a}$_{se}$^{ru}t$_{tel}$ _____

3 Circle the correct words.

1 Humpback whales migrate for the first time with their
fathers / **mothers**.

2 The **male** / **female** penguin keeps its new egg warm.

3 The penguin often does not eat for up to **6** / **16** weeks
when it is keeping the egg warm.

4 Fish move away from coral reefs to **feed** / **hide**.

5 Billions of animals make **vertical** / **altitudinal** migrations
in the ocean every day.

4 Complete the puzzle.

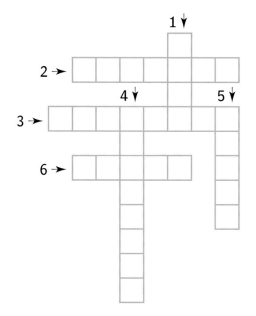

1 Large fish that migrate up to 10,500 kilometers between places.

2 A bird that migrates across the Antarctic to breed.

3 A species of whale that sings a song when it is migrating.

4 Small animals and plants that live in the ocean.

5 Very small animals that whales eat.

6 An animal with sharp teeth that migrates up and down the ocean.

5 Answer the questions.

1 How far do humpback whales go when they migrate?

_____

2 Why do whales migrate to warm oceans in winter?

_____

3 Why do whales migrate to cold oceans in summer?

_____

4 Why do reef fish lay their eggs near the edge of the reef?

_____

5 Why do animal plankton move up the ocean at night?

_____

7 Going Home to Breed

← Read pages 28–31.

1 Complete the sentences. Then write the numbers.

migrate breed hatch adult ocean

1 Salmon eggs _____.

2 The young salmon _____ down rivers to the ocean.

3 They live in the _____ for a few years.

4 The _____ salmon migrate up rivers.

5 They _____ and then die.

young rivers ocean larvae

6 Eel _____ move across the ocean with ocean currents.

7 The _____ eels migrate up rivers and streams.

8 The eels live in _____ for many years.

9 They migrate back to the _____ to breed.

2 **Match.**

1 Salmon	hunt salmon when they swim up rivers.
2 Bears	lay their eggs on land.
3 Eels	migrate from the ocean to rivers to breed.
4 Sea turtles	migrate from rivers to the ocean to breed.

3 **Complete the sentences.**

ocean sand land ocean

1 Sea turtles lay their eggs on _____ and they cover them with sand.

2 Then they go back to the _____ .

3 When they hatch, the young turtles dig their way out of the _____ .

4 Then they go into the _____ .

4 **Answer the questions.**

1 How do salmon find their way when they migrate?

_____

2 What happens to sockeye salmon before they breed?

_____

3 What helps salmon to swim over dams?

_____

4 What happens to eels when they move from fresh water to salt water?

_____

8 Changing Migrations

← Read pages 32–35.

1 Complete the chart.

> trees   power lines   ice on polar oceans   deserts
> wind turbines   fishing   ponds   storms
> ocean currents   hunting   dams   roads   fences

1 Migrants like tuna and sea turtles are in danger because of:

_____ or _____

2 Animals sometimes cannot migrate because of:

_____   _____   _____

3 Habitats are damaged because people:

cut down _____

take out _____

build _____

build _____

4 Journeys are more dangerous for migrants now because:

there are more _____

there is less _____

_____ are getting bigger

_____ are changing

2 Complete the sentences.

> Polar bears   willow warbler   Cod   seals   albatrosses

1 Every year, many _____ are killed by fishing hooks.

2 Birds like the _____ are staying in the north for longer than usual.

3 _____ migrate from the ice to the land in summer.

4 Because the ice is melting earlier in spring, polar bears have less time for catching _____ .

5 _____ are in danger from too much fishing.

3 Answer the questions.

1 Why is Earth getting too warm?

_____

2 Why do scientists think that many animal species will migrate to new places or stop migrating?

_____

3 Where do polar bears live in winter?

_____

4 Why has the climate changing made it difficult for polar bears to migrate to land?

_____

5 Why are scientists putting special markers on some migrants?

_____

A Migrants Poster

1 Complete the charts for these migrant animals.

Name:	Monarch Butterfly
What does it look like?	
How far does it migrate?	
Migrates from:	
Migrates to:	
Interesting fact:	

Name:	Reindeer
What does it look like?	
How far does it migrate?	
Migrates from:	
Migrates to:	
Interesting fact:	

2 Choose two more migrant animals. Complete the charts.

Name:	
What does it look like?	
How far does it migrate?	
Migrates from:	
Migrates to:	
Interesting fact:	

Name:	
What does it look like?	
How far does it migrate?	
Migrates from:	
Migrates to:	
Interesting fact:	

3 Make a poster. Write sentences about the migrant animals and add pictures. Display your poster.

A Migration Diary

1 Write the names of some animals that migrate to, from, or through your country.

2 Complete the chart. Try to do this for a whole year!

Name of animal:	What does it look like?	Where did you see it? When?	Where did you see it? When?	Where did you see it? When?

Glossary

adult a person or animal that has finished growing

alone without any other people or animals

attack to fight with someone or something

bear a large wild animal

breed to have babies

buffalo (*plural* **buffaloes**) a large animal like a cow

carry to take something to another place

change to become different; to make something different

chemical a solid or liquid that is made by chemistry

climate the usual type of weather in a place

coast the land beside the sea or ocean

cod a large ocean fish that people eat

compass something that helps you find the way north, south, east, or west

coral reef a long line of small, bright animals that look like rocks in the ocean

cover to be over something

crop a plant that we grow in large amounts

cross to move from one side to another

current large amounts of warm or cold water that move around the ocean

dam it's built across a river to stop water

damage to make something bad or weak

danger when something could hurt or kill people or animals

dawn the time of day when you first see light

deep going a long way down

deer (*plural* **deer**) a wild animal

die to stop living

dig to make a hole in the ground

double to get two times bigger

echo a sound that comes back

edge the outside of something

energy we need energy to move and grow; machines need energy to work

enough how much we want or need

escape to get away

feather the soft parts that cover a bird

female a woman or girl; an animal that can lay eggs or have babies

fence it goes around land to keep animals in or out

flood when a place becomes covered with water

follow to go after somebody or something

forest a place with a lot of trees

fresh not old (for food or grass)

gas not a solid or liquid; like air

gazelle an animal like a deer

goat an animal with a hairy coat

grass a green plant

group a number of people or things that are together

grow to get bigger

habitat the place where an animal or plant normally lives

half one of two parts

hatch to come out of an egg

herder someone who controls a herd or group of animals

hide to go somewhere where you will not be seen

hook a rounded, sharp thing used for catching fish

huge very big

hurt to give pain

hyena a wild animal like a dog

insect a very small animal with six legs

jellyfish an ocean animal with long, thin parts like arms

kill to make someone or something die

krill very small ocean animals with shells

ladder you use it to climb up and down

lake a big area of water

larva (*plural* **larvae**) a young animal that looks different from its parent; it changes when it becomes an adult

lay eggs to produce eggs

leopard a wild animal from the cat family

lichen a very small plant that grows on rocks or trees

magnetic field an area around something with a force that pulls some metals toward it

male a man or boy; an animal that cannot usually have babies

mammal an animal that has babies and feeds its babies milk; people are mammals

marker it shows what something is

mate an animal that another animal has babies with

melt to become liquid because of being hot

move to go from one place to another

muscle a part of your body that you contract or relax to move your bones

ocean the salt water that covers most of Earth

opposite different

plain a large area of flat land

plankton very small animals and plants that live in the ocean

polar near the North Pole or South Pole

polluted made dirty

pollution something that makes air, land, or water dirty

pond a small area of water

power line a thick wire that carries electricity

power station a building where electricity is made

protect to keep safe from danger

push to make something move away

reach to get to

rest to do little or nothing after working

river water on land that goes to the ocean

road vehicles travel on it

safe not in danger

seal an ocean mammal that eats fish

shape for example, circle, square, triangle

shark a large ocean fish

sheep (*plural* **sheep**) an animal that we raise for wool and meat

silver a shiny gray color

skin the part of an animal that covers the outside of the body

skyscraper a very tall building in a city

special different and important

species a group of the same type of animal

starve to become ill or die because you do not have enough to eat

storm bad weather; lots of wind and rain

stream a small river

thicker less thin

tiring making you feel tired

tropical from the Tropics

tunnel a long hole under the ground

vehicle something for transporting things or people

way a route or road that you take to get somewhere

weigh if you weigh something you see how heavy it is

weight how heavy something is

wet season the time of year in the Tropics when there is a lot of rain

wind turbine a tall machine that makes energy from the wind

wing birds and planes have wings to help them to fly

without not having something; not doing something

wolf (*plural* **wolves**) a wild animal in the dog family

young baby animals

Oxford Read and Discover

Series Editor: Hazel Geatches • CLIL Adviser: John Clegg

Oxford Read and Discover graded readers are at four levels, from 3 to 6, suitable for students from age 8 and older. They cover many topics within three subject areas, and can support English across the curriculum, or Content and Language Integrated Learning (CLIL).

Available for each reader:
• Audio CD Pack (book & audio CD)
• Activity Book

For Teacher's Notes & CLIL Guidance go to
www.oup.com/elt/teacher/readanddiscover

Subject Area / Level	The World of Science & Technology	The Natural World	The World of Arts & Social Studies
③ 600 headwords	• How We Make Products • Sound and Music • Super Structures • Your Five Senses	• Amazing Minibeasts • Animals in the Air • Life in Rainforests • Wonderful Water	• Festivals Around the World • Free Time Around the World
④ 750 headwords	• All About Plants • How to Stay Healthy • Machines Then and Now • Why We Recycle	• All About Desert Life • All About Ocean Life • Animals at Night • Incredible Earth	• Animals in Art • Wonders of the Past
⑤ 900 headwords	• Materials to Products • Medicine Then and Now • Transportation Then and Now • Wild Weather	• All About Islands • Animal Life Cycles • Exploring Our World • Great Migrations	• Homes Around the World • Our World in Art
⑥ 1,050 headwords	• Cells and Microbes • Clothes Then and Now • Incredible Energy • Your Amazing Body	• All About Space • Caring for Our Planet • Earth Then and Now • Wonderful Ecosystems	• Helping Around the World • Food Around the World

For younger students, **Dolphin Readers** Levels Starter, 1, and 2 are available.